ANGEL in the NURSERY:
Destiny Fulfilled

ANGEL in the NURSERY:
Destiny Fulfilled

A Mother's Memoir on How She Stopped the
Transmission of Intergenerational Trauma

DANNA PERDUE-MELTON
Foreword by Trinity Perdue

XULON PRESS

Xulon Press
2301 Lucien Way #415
Maitland, FL 32751
407.339.4217
www.xulonpress.com

Unless otherwise indicated, Scripture quotations taken from the
Holy Bible, New International Version (NIV). Copyright © 1973,
1978, 1984, 2011 by Biblica, Inc.™. Used by permission. All rights
reserved.

Printed in the United States of America.

Paperback ISBN-13: 978-1-66280-964-4

Dedication:

This book is dedicated to my mom, and all the mothers that really strive to be exceptional mothers but just don't know how. You were the sweetest mom / grandmas a girl could ever have. I love you and miss you dearly.

Table of Contents

Acknowledgement

I WOULD LIKE to give all the honor and glory to God. God has transformed my life into something beautiful, and for that I am eternally grateful. I would like to thank my family and friends for all your love and support throughout the years. It hasn't been easy, but we made it to higher ground. I would like to send a special thanks to Trinity Yael Perdue: you inspire me to be all that I can be, and I am honored that God chose me to be your mother. Special thanks to Alice Owens, my personal angel in the nursery, and Chris Davidson—when I had no hope of retrieving the only copy of this book from a broken flash drive, you made it happen. Lastly, thanks to all the children and families I have had the opportunity to work with over the years. You continue to show me that with God, anything is possible.

Foreword

AFRICAN AMERICAN AND female: a "double minority," some would say; a life filled with physical and emotional barriers, disadvantages and suffering at every corner. For what the world proclaimed for me as destiny, God said no. My mother has always told me of God's promise to her about my life, and to say that He has kept His promise would be an understatement. I cannot pretend to understand or even visualize the kind of life my mother lived before me, but I will forever be in awe of her strength and courage. She admits to me she was truly lost and, as a child, experienced some things that no child ever should. It's hard to hear her words, but they stand as constant reaffirmations that our lives truly could have been different. Although her stories are foreign to me, I appreciate them because they are pieces of herself, she did not have to share. Being a black single mother, a predicament I'm sure no one wishes for themselves, she filled me with love, life, and laughter. By the grace of God, what I saw and what was couldn't have been farther apart. Our physical conditions were overshadowed by the love that I received from the people God brought into my life. And as I grow older and reflect on my life, I realize the greatest gift was getting to know God. He helped my mother lay the groundwork, but the choice was ultimately mine. Without His leadership and guidance, I understand I would be forfeiting His purpose for my life. I am by no means perfect, yet God continues to bless me and my life. It is because of His words and unconditional love that I feel empowered and excited about my future. I can omit what the world says about me, because God's words are very clear. I pray that this book will not only be a blessing to others, but that God has guided my mother and used her as a vessel to share His Word.

Preface

THIS BOOK IS inspired by Titus 2:3 (NIV), which simply states, "Likewise teach the older women to be reverent in the way they live, not to be slanderers or addicted to much wine, but to teach what is good." I believe this Scripture encourages women to live their lives in a way that honors God. This Scripture reminds me of my early adult years, filled with clubs, parties, and drinks. I wish I had an aged woman to help me adjust to the demands of early adulthood; someone who understood my struggle and pain; someone who would not only talk the talk but walk the walk. As a child, I experienced some harsh conditions that stemmed from poverty and domestic violence. I saw and heard things that would eventually have a negative impact on my life. These experiences shaped the way I viewed myself, my environment, and others. As I continued my journey, I became pregnant. This was a turning point for me, and my life was forever changed. If any of this resonates with you, this book is for you. Allow me to be that aged woman, a teacher of good things... This book is not about being a perfect parent; instead, it will give you some useful tools on how to be a successful parent. No matter what you have been through or are currently encountering, you can make it. I am confident that success is an option because I achieved it. As I share my story of trials and triumphs, it is my hope and prayer that this book is instrumental in sparking a movement towards a better understanding of what our children need to not only survive but thrive.

A Gift from God

Twenty years later, I would have never imagined that my gift from God would come in such a tiny packet; six pounds and seven ounces. The day Trinity was born was bittersweet. After my labor and delivery, I learned that my grandmother, affectionately known as Dear Dear, had passed away. I can vividly remember the day Trinity was born. I was up late on the phone with her dad, fussing over God knows what, when I heard a pop. My water broke! In a panic, I screamed to the rest of my family, "It's time!" As the time approached for Trinity to make her entrance into this world, I couldn't help but think about my childhood and all the horrific things I witnessed. I vowed I would protect and educate Trinity, but like many first-time single parents, I didn't really realize what it was going to take to raise a child on my own. Trinity's father and I had the best intentions at trying to stay connected, but as time went on, it became clear we were not going to be together.

Things began to get real as her father made an exit, with no intentions to return until she was old enough to visit on her own, or so he said. At any rate, our lives went on; Trinity began to grow into a sweet little girl. As I tried to raise Trinity, I was smacked in the face with the realization that I needed raising myself. I was always told what to do, but never taught how to do it. Life had dealt me a very difficult hand, but I was determined that I wouldn't let my past prevent me from being a good mother. As a matter of fact, it inspired me to be the best mother I could be at whatever cost. Psalm 127:3 states, " Children are a blessing and a gift from Lord" (CEV). Trinity didn't seem like a gift at first, and it took some time renewing my mind with the Word of God before I could truly understand what that really meant. As gifts from God, mothers and fathers should value their children and teach them how to love themselves as well as others. It is our job to train them in the way they should go, which will lead to life and not death. Lastly, as parents, we should be positive role models for our children. It is not enough to tell our children what to do; we must be examples for them. It is very important to practice what you preach in front of your children. Anything else is hypocrisy; actions are so much more important than words. Take some time to reflect on what you have just read and your own childhood. As you reflect, write down how you felt as a child. Reflect on your relationship with your child and how you envision them as he/she learns and grows.

REFLECTION

_____

_____

_____

_____

_____

_____

_____

_____

_____

_____

_____

_____

_____

_____

_____

_____

YOU KNIT ME TOGETHER IN MY MOTHER'S WOMB —
PSALM 139:13

YOU ARE NOT ALONE

ACCORDING TO NEW research conducted by the Pew Research Center, approximately a fourth of U.S. children under the age of eighteen live with a single parent or no other adult. This is at a rate of twenty-three percent and more than three times the rate of children around the world (Kramer, S., 2019).

This statistic symbolizes a lot of different things to people living in poverty. This could mean low-income housing, a lack of resources, poor healthcare, and education. These conditions can lead to isolation, sickness, and even death. The amount of stress in these households is harsh and has life-long consequences. A study conducted in 1995 by the American health maintenance organization Kaiser Permanente and the Centers for Disease Control and Prevention revealed an association between stressful traumatic childhood experiences and early death (CDC, 2016). The study results suggest that household dysfunction in childhood contributes to health problems years later. The numbers of adverse childhood experiences are strongly connected with risky health behaviors, such as smoking, alcohol and drug abuse, promiscuity, and severe obesity. According to the Substance Abuse and Mental Health Administration, the ACE study found that adverse childhood experiences are common and often occur together (SAMHSA, 2020).

So, exactly what are adverse childhood experiences? They include household dysfunction, such as witnessing domestic violence or growing up with family members who have substance abuse disorders. ACE also include:

- Physical abuse

- Sexual abuse
- Emotional abuse
- Physical neglect
- Emotional neglect
- Substance misuse within household
- Household mental illness
- Parental separation or divorce
- Incarcerated household member

I was overwhelmed the first time I saw the ACE study questionnaire. As I answered the questions, I realized that I had experienced more than half of the childhood traumas. My mother was a sweet lady, but she had a very serious drug addiction. My father is a Vietnam War vet and struggles with mental illness and addiction. I was exposed to domestic violence and my father was incarcerated for most of my early childhood. These types of stress and trauma really altered the way I viewed myself and my environment.

The world wasn't a safe place to me. As a child, I was very nervous all the time and worried about my mom. By high school, I was a heavy drinker and in an abusive relationship. I had very poor coping skills and honestly believed that love and violence were one and the same. I engaged in some very risky behaviors, and I am grateful to be alive today. My early childhood experiences led to not only risky behaviors, but to low self-esteem and fear. This caused me considerable pain and grief during my adolescence and early adult years, to the point of considering suicide. It is only by the grace of God that I am still here to tell you that things can change, and to let you know you are not alone or crazy… nor any other labels people will try to give you. There is hope and healing available, but you must want more out of life than what you are getting. Raising my daughter in a single-parent home wasn't easy, and we faced several challenges. I had to make some hard choices and I chose life. The Scripture says, in Deuteronomy 30:15-18, "Today I am giving you a choice. You can choose life and success or death and disaster. I am commanding you to be loyal to the Lord, to live the way He has told you, and to obey His laws and teachings" (CEV).

It wasn't always easy to do the right thing, especially if you were taught to do the opposite. I'm not perfect, and I have done my share of dirt. Eventually I got sick and tired of being sick and tired. I had to put the childish things away and be the responsible adult that my daughter needed me to be.

This process would include eliminating risky behaviors, bad habits, and traditions that I had picked up along the way. I had to learn how to love myself and, in the process, learn how to love others. I had to be **woke** about my current situation and the conditions that have plagued my community for decades. I had to be a part of the solution, instead of a part of the problem. Finally, I had to change my mind about the direction in which I was heading. The drinking and drugs had to go; I had to find a better way of coping with life's difficulties. I had to let go of all the nonproductive relationships that hindered my growth. There is a saying that if you lie, you will cheat, and if you cheat, you will steal. What we do is so very important regarding our children. They do what we do, and they say what we say. Our children are always there watching us, and if we have no moral values our children will not develop the respect, they need for themselves and others. Over the years I have observed people that did not value themselves or others, and they usually settle for less than what they deserve and take life for granted.

You have a unique opportunity to raise your child or children differently than how you were raised. But to do so will require you to think differently, change your behavior patterns, and even abandon some things you were taught. Successful parenting begins with you… it is a conscious decision to change the way in which you live to ensure that your child has a better and more fruitful life. Before you move on to the next chapter, please take time and reflect on what you just read. What are some things you have experienced or learned that affect your current thinking? What are some habits you want to change in your life?

REFLECTION

LISTEN TO ADVICE AND ACCEPT INSTRUCTION, AND IN THE END, YOU WILL BE WISE. — PROVERBS 19:2

POVERTY AND TOXIC STRESS

ON A MORE practical level, we all have needs. In looking at
Maslow's hierarchy of needs, there are levels of needs that we
all maneuver through. According to Abraham Maslow (1943),
people are motivated to achieve certain needs, and some needs
take priority over others (McLeod, S., 2018). For example, the
most basic need is for physical survival. Once the first level is

fulfilled, we are motivated to the next level and so on. It is very hard to teach a skill that you have not already mastered. For example, when I had my daughter, I hadn't secured resources for myself, such as transportation and housing. I was living with my aunt and I had to get someone to take me everywhere I had to go; this was a major blow to my independence. I couldn't reach the next phase of my development until I was able to move through the security stage. I see a lot of this with the families I encounter.

A large portion of my clients' experience poverty and chronic stress. They are unable to move successful through these stages, and it can be exhausting. Chronic stress can take on many forms; this stress is continual and seems to never end. The biggest stressors are financial worries and unsafe communities. To have a strong community, we must teach our children how to successfully move through these stages. This means educating ourselves, building up our communities, and teaching the next generation to do the same.

Now, I never said that this would be easy, but it is well worth it. As I began to grow and develop, I was able to work and go to school. During that time in my life, my first order of business involved gaining my independence. I really struggled to get my driver's license, and after lots of prayer and practice,

I was able to overcome my fear. I worked a full-time job and attended college at the University of Alabama at Birmingham. Again, this was a process, and it took lots of dedication and hard work. It felt like an eternity, but eventually graduation came in 2008. Not only was I able to graduate but, I had purchased my own home months before graduation. I said all of that to say this; we must have some type of balance in our lives. We cannot continue to worry about things we cannot control. We must set realistic goals for ourselves. What are your talents and dreams? Do you have a plan for your life? Where do you see yourself in the next five to ten years? These are some questions you need to ask yourself. Planning can alleviate some of the unnecessary stress in your life. Excessive stress and worry are harmful and can lead to mental and physical problems. As I mentioned before, I constantly worried as a child. I experienced depression and suicidal thoughts in high school and developed a fear of driving. Excessive stress and worry can also lead to physical ailments, such as weight gain and loss, headaches, hair loss, and even death. When in session with parents or training on self-care, I always present this scenario.

Now imagine this scenario: You are on an airplane. There's a bunch of turbulence, the plane is shuddering, and everyone is in a panic. The oxygen masks drop down from the ceiling, and you have a child with you. Question: Who do you put the oxygen mask on first? Child or yourself? The answer to this question is very simple. When you fly on an airplane, the flight attendant instructs you to put your oxygen mask on first, before helping others. Why is this an important rule for ensuring survival? Because if you run out of oxygen, you can't help anyone else with their oxygen masks. This is an important metaphor for those of you who run around taking care of everything and everyone else except yourself. If you don't take care of yourself, you can experience burnout, fatigue, reduced mental effectiveness, health problems, anxiety, and frustration. So, what does this have to do with parent-child relationships? Providing care to children, especially young children, is an intense and demanding job.

Parents and teachers are under pressure to meet the demands of running a household/classroom, personal concerns, and responding to the child/children in their care. Stress is natural and can be inevitable, but stress can take a toll on your health and effectiveness as a parent or provider. Stress doesn't just affect you; it also impacts the child/children in your care. During an online training provided by the Center for Early Childhood Mental Health Consultation, I learned that several forms of severe discipline and neglect occur because caregivers are stressed and may have an insufficient support system in place to manage their stressors in a healthy way (ECMHC, 2020). Before you continue, please take a moment to reflect on what you just read. What are your constant stressors? How can you find balance?

REFLECTION

THOSE WHO LIVE IN THE SHELTER OF THE MOST HIGH WILL FIND REST IN THE SHADOW OF THE ALMIGHTY. — PSALM 91:1

THE GHOST IN THE NURSERY

DURING MY STUDIES, I came across some very significant terms that shaped my thinking. Ghost in the Nursery is a metaphor used when looking at a parent/caregiver and

19

child relationship. In her paper "Ghosts in the Nursery," Selma Fraiberg discusses the "emotional baggage" parents and other caregivers may carry from their own experiences of being parented, including conflicted feelings about their parents, a sense of being unsupported in childhood, and traumatizing memories (Liberman et al., 2005). The ghosts often negatively impact simple things, such as feeding, sleep, toilet training, and discipline. For me, those ghosts represent those things we do just because our parents or grandparents did them. We dare not question these habits and, in doing so, pass on the ghost or emotional baggage to our children. As a child, I was told that little girls should be seen and not heard. This statement gave great emphasis to the outward beauties while neglecting all the inward attributes, leaving the voices of doubt, rejection, and frustration to fester. It's hard when you don't know where you come from; it's even harder when you don't know where you are going. I have stumbled upon several ghosts in the work that I do with parents, caregivers, and teachers.

There is a transmission of numbing silence that has been passed from one generation to the next. Unrealistic expectations are being set for children of all ages. Children are expected to do things that some adults haven't even achieved. They are not taught how to love themselves or how to get along with others.

These unrealistic expectations lead to the ideas that children are misbehaving and require some tough love. Tough love comes in many different forms, but the most common form is corporal punishment. Corporal punishment is one ghost that has evolved throughout time and has a disturbing effect on the parent-child/caregiver relationship. I can remember my mother as she recalled some of her own childhood experiences, in which it was common for parents to discipline their children with an extension cord. I can remember thinking to myself, *that's a bit harsh*. But to my surprise, as I talk with other adults around my mother's age and older, this custom was a common form of discipline in many African American homes.

Discipline should have balance. I have learned that corporal punishment is ineffective and promotes violence toward others. In 2012, Brookings Institution reported that more than seventy percent of Americans agreed that "it is sometimes necessary to discipline a child with a good, hard spanking." Children spanked regularly and/or severely are at higher risk for mental health problems, ranging from anxiety to depression to alcohol and drug abuse (Cuddy, E., & Reeves, R.V. (2014). My personal experience with corporal punishment led to a severe fear of driving. My grandmother left me in a running car when I was very young. As a curious child, I pulled the gear and the car began to roll backward, almost hitting a pole. My grand-mother, mother, and aunt all gave me a good whooping for that, but they also instilled in me a fear that would shape my life. I had a fear of driving and didn't get my license until the age of twenty-five. Some people may argue that it was my fault, that I should've known not to touch the gear, while others would say my grandmother was in error for leaving me in a running car. This is an extreme case of corporal punishment that hindered my growth process.

I have seen parents put more emphasis on clothes and shoes than their children. Materialism has replaced nurturing and loving parents that children need. First Peter 3:3-4 (NLT) states, "You should clothe yourselves instead within the beauty that comes from within, the unfading beauty of a gentle and quiet spirit which is precious to God." I believe that this lack of nurturance and love, in combination with an emphasis on material things, has led to the violence in the black commu-nity. These behaviors are learned and exist in and outside of the home. This self-hatred is further perpetuated through social constructs, such as impoverished neighborhoods, failing schools, and the media.

There are several things we, as parents, can do to protect our children as they learn and grow. This process of growth starts at home. As our children's first teachers, we have an obligation to provide them with some life skills. Many parents lack the necessary life skills to pass on to their children, thus leaving them vulnerable and unable to lead productive lives. Before you continue, please take a moment to reflect on what you just read. What are some conflicting memories or feelings you have about your childhood? How do these memories or feelings affect how you parent your child?

REFLECTION

_____

_____

_____

_____

_____

_____

_____

_____

_____

_____

_____

_____

_____

DO NOT REMEMBER THE FORMER THINGS OR PONDER THE THINGS OF THE PAST. — ISAIAH 43:18

THE ANGEL IN THE NURSERY

"ANGEL IN THE Nursery" is another metaphor used to examine the experiences between a parent and a child, where the child feels understood, accepted, and loved (Liebermann et al., 2005). The angels are those experiences that work against the ghost. For me, the angel was in the nursery in more ways than one. My first real job started out in a nursery. I worked as a preschool teacher for over fifteen years and I loved every minute of it.

I have worked in every room with every age group. I treasure these moments because the nursery was a place where I was able to grow and learn how to raise my own daughter. As I look back, I can remember the training I attended on how to care for very young children. I observed how the mothers and fathers handled their kids with care, love, and compassion.

I also encountered an angel in the nursery at my church. I will never forget that day; it was the day I gave my life to the Lord. I can remember feeling nervous and uneasy. I was worried about my daughter Trinity. I had experienced so many horrible things and wanted to provide Trinity with a better life, but I knew I didn't know how. I was in desperate need of guidance and prayed that God would help me as I tried to raise my daughter on my own. One day, as I entered the nursery at my church, one of the workers approached me as I brought Trinity into the nursery. She said, "You know you don't have to worry about Trinity." In that moment of unbelief and awe, I stood there and looked at the lady. She said that God is going to take care of Trinity's every need. As I began to sob, the lady led me into the salvation prayer and my life was forever changed. Things weren't always perfect after that moment, but I knew God had heard my cry for help.

As I continued to attend regular worship and prayer services, my mindset began to change. One day, God spoke to me in a small, still voice and told me who I was in Him. He let me know that I was perfectly and wonderfully made. Trinity and I were on our way to wholeness. I was no longer defined by my past; I had a new identity in God and my life was changed forever. Trinity has grown up to be a very fine young lady.

God made good on His promises. He has made a way for Trinity that is over and above what I could imagine or even think. He even provided us with an extended family through a local community center in our hometown of Birmingham, Alabama. It was in this place that we were able to experience a community of love, acceptance, and even forgiveness. Your life can change as well. When things look dim and you don't know what to do, God is always there. Pray and seek guidance. God will meet you right where you are, but you must be willing to do something different. It is possible to have a loving and enriching relationship with your child, even if you didn't have that type of relationship with your mother or father. This will require some time and commitment, but it is possible. Before you continue, please take a moment to reflect on what you just read. Focus your attention on some good moments you have had and how they have inspired you. Who are the angels in your life?

REFLECTION

_____

_____

_____

_____

_____

_____

_____

_____

_____

_____

_____

_____

_____

_____

_____

BE NOT FORGETFUL TO ENTERTAIN STRANGERS: FOR
THEREBY SOME HAVE ENTERTAINED ANGELS UNAWARES.
— HEBREWS 13:2

A New Generation

I WASN'T PREPARED for motherhood when I got pregnant with Trinity and I knew it. I kept a pregnancy journal, and the first page reads, "November 17, 1999 was the first time I was able to hear my baby's heartbeat. At ten and a half weeks, my baby seems strong. From the time I found out that I was pregnant until that very moment, I was afraid something would or was wrong. But it appears everything is going to be fine. God blessed me with life and at that moment, when I heard that little heartbeat, I knew everything would be alright. It was a remarkable experience and reassurance that I had life inside me. And I hope and pray that everything keeps going well. Since the pregnancy began, I've begun to change for the good. I've begun to get closer to my family and learn to try to do for myself, since I'll have a bigger responsibility soon. So, I'm trying harder, more than ever to achieve some type of independence. It will be good for me and my new baby, as well as the father. I thank God every night for my little miracle."

As I read through my pregnancy journal, and look how far Trinity and I have come, I am amazed at our progress. As I grew, so did Trinity. She is an extraordinary young lady and student. She is very confident in who she is and has excelled in ways I could have only imagined. In reading a paper she recently wrote; I was amazed how her memories shaped her into the person she is today. As I was completing this book, I came across a paper Trinity wrote about herself during her senior year titled "Who Am I?" I would like to share this paper with you and encourage you today. You can raise a child that knows who he/she is and where he/she is going. You can raise a leader; strong men and women that have a sense of self-worth and how to treat others. You can raise your children to be successful despite poverty, negative stereotypes, and injustice that plague our neighborhoods and communities.

In reading Trinity's essay, I was amazed by her self-perception and outlook. Trinity's view was significantly different from her reality. She took great pride in her family's strengths. Trinity considered herself middle class; she never thought of herself as being poor. Trinity was named 2017 QuestBridge College Match Scholarship recipient. This is a very prestigious, national program that pairs high-achieving high school seniors from low-income households with full scholarships to the nation's top colleges. It is an extremely competitive process and from a pool of 15,606 applicants, only 918 outstanding students were selected. Students chosen for College Match are admitted early with a guaranteed full, four-year scholarship, including tuition, room and board, and other expenses. Trinity enrolled as a 2018 QuestBridge Scholar at Washington and Lee University in Lexington, Virginia. I must stop right here and take a praise break. God has been so faithful, and this is an example that He will provide all our needs.

I will admit that in thinking about my daughter's future, I never imagined that she would be a QuestBridge College Match Scholarship recipient. Looking at my childhood, I was glad I made it through high school, let alone college. To see the fruits of my labor is very rewarding, but to have a promise from God makes this even more special. God is not a respecter of persons; this means He doesn't treat people according to their status or importance. Success is only a prayer away. Say this prayer: "Dear God, I come to You in the name of Jesus. I admit that I am not right with You, and I want to be right with You. I ask You to forgive me of my sins. I believe with my heart, and I confess with my mouth, that Jesus is the Lord and Savior of my life. Thank you for saving me! Now, help me to live for You the rest of this life. In the name of Jesus, I pray. Amen."

I would like to welcome you into the family of God! I encourage you to find a church home and continue your journey with the Lord. Take some time to reflect on what you just read and let it be a reminder of the day you gave your life to God.

REFLECTION

_____

_____

_____

_____

_____

_____

_____

_____

_____

_____

_____

_____

_____

_____

THE GODLY WALK WITH INTEGRITY; BLESSED ARE THEIR CHILDREN WHO FOLLOW THEM. — PROVERBS 20:7

Trinity Yael Perdue

Who Am I? Who am I? Every year, during elementary and middle school, I participated in the wax museum my school held during Black History Month. Every student was required to choose an African American that stood out to them, compose a biographical speech, and dress up as his/her selected individual. I can remember always being excited about the assignment, but nervous about my ability to memorize my speech. I usually elected an African American that I thought would be unfamiliar to my peers. My favorite was always Mamie Clark, partially because she was my mom's favorite psychologist and partially because her "Brown Study" helped to heavily influence the ruling that would end segregation. It was always so easy for me to flip the switch and share their story as if it was my own. It was so much easier than sharing details about myself, because they were facts that could not be doubted or questioned. When I talk about myself, a similar kind of confidence stems from the conversation, but a very critical nature also comes along with it. This critical nature could come in the form of doubt, regret, or even omitting aspects about myself that I think people may dislike. Either way, I look forward to learning more about myself and sharing what aspects have influenced who I am in this cultural study. First, I would like to start by saying that there is nothing that I would change about my name. It matches me perfectly and sheds a lot of light into who I am. The name "Trinity" embodies my Christian identity. It means the unity of the Father, Son, and Holy Spirit as three persons in one Godhead, according to Christian dogma. "Yael" showcases my multicultural background and upbringing, with the Hebrew name meaning strength of God. Finally, my last name "Perdue" traces a long line of family history on my mother's side of the family. It is because of my name that I was influenced to divide my cultural study into three major sections that highlight these areas of my life.

My mother first heard the name "Trinity" watching the movie *The Matrix*. She loved Trinity's fierce character and decided that this was the name for me after researching its meaning. She would always tell me that I was a major turning point in her life. I have a better relationship with my dad now, but my mother was the one who raised me. Now that I am older, I am able to appreciate her more and understand the importance of the individual time I had with my mom, as she helped to mold my character. The one thing that I will always admire about her, and hope to have one day, is her grit and fierce demeanor. I used to always say, "Stop trying to psychoanalyze me; I am not one of your patients," because I thought a lot of what she did and knew as a counselor translated into how she raised me. Once I got older, I was able to understand that my mom knew what was best for me and her past experiences, as well as what she studied in college, were more of aides in raising me. She has always let her actions speak louder than her words and she has always been very organized. I think a lot of my political views have been influenced by her and her desire to break the stereotypes that come with African Americans. She has always felt that society is not meant to benefit African Americans, but also that this cycle of poverty is fed by the lack of education and understanding amongst African Americans. We could talk for hours about broad topics such as these and love to share ideas with each other. I would not change a thing about how my mother raised me or the invaluable lessons she taught me. "I can do all things through Christ which strengthens me" (Phil. 4:13, KJV). This was one of my first Scriptures that I learned, and I memorized as a child. I was introduced to Christianity through Bible stories and going to church with my mom. Christianity is not just something that I do or believe in, but it is who I am. If my mom has not taught me anything else, she has taught me how essential my relationship with God is and the importance of my consistency with my faith. It is because of Christianity that I have morals of kindness and integrity. I give all my troubles to God and rely on Him as my provider. Whenever I am stressed and worried, praying and reading Scripture helps to instill me with confidence and happiness. It has always been important to me to acknowledge that my mother never forced me into Christianity. She gave me the tools and introduced me, but I am now at the age where I can say it is my choice. Baptism is an essential part of being saved, and I am thankful that my mom elected to give me the choice when I got older versus baptizing me as a baby. She always gave me the freedom to explore and find my own identity in Christ.

Looking more into my personality, I have two sides. I am either vibrantly scattered all over the place or I am reserved, and there is no in-between. I always joke that it is because my zodiac sign is Gemini. The vibrantly scattered me is very talkative and funny. You can find me dancing in the halls and cracking jokes. I always love making up my own catchphrases and making other people laugh. This side of me is free to wonder and explore. I am most independent and active during this time. On the other hand, the other side of me can be quiet and cautious. I would like to think that I am also independent in this aspect, as I feed off of other people's energy and elect when I want to include myself. In the past, teachers have asked me to be more vocal and assertive, and I have really tried to participate more in class this year. In this, I have found that I hate being contained when I do participate and struggle with remaining open. I think I have always been quiet and reserved growing up, and this year I am allowing myself to be expressed through the very scattered side of me. I have found that when I am upset or stressed, I resort back to the quiet and reserved for control. This is how I have always coped with my emotions. My mom is the complete opposite, as she is more vocal and assertive. Veering into the more cultural aspects that have influenced me, a question that I have always taken joy in answering is "What is your middle name?" It is fun telling people my middle name and how to pronounce it, as people usually pronounce it as "Yale." "Are you Jewish?" is the question that immediately follows. My response is always no, but I joke that I am about ten percent Jewish. I attended a Jewish preschool until I started kindergarten, and that experience helped to expose me to different cultures. I never felt hatred or looked down at my peers because of their religious beliefs. I was excited to learn about beliefs that were important to them, and I was able to accept our differences as something that made us unique and interesting. This also made me feel a part of their culture, in some respects, as I learned the significance of keeping kosher, studied many Jewish holidays, and memorized all the Shabbat prayers.

I have always been middle class, and I feel that this has taught me worth of a dollar and instilled in me the importance of hard work. My mom always made me work toward something I wanted. Everyone in my family knows that I always have money. As a kid, I was huge on saving and I was very stingy. I absolutely hated spending money and usually tried to challenge myself to see how much I could save. I think one aspect I have come to understand about myself is that I don't like change. I have never been good with transitioning into stages of life. I look forward to the future, but I hate aging. On a similar note, I have always hated the stereotypes that have come with being a female. My mom raised me to be a confident individual and I have always taken pride in being female. I hated that women were seen as lesser and more emotional compared to men. This may be one of the reasons that I try to show as little emotion as possible and usually revert to quietness over expressing myself.

My "Clash" gender presentation has definitely helped me to better understand the common behaviors of women and why each gender acts the way they do. I think a lot of my love of culture stems from my experiences at an early age. My mom was always making sure that I knew how special and unique I was. I grew up having dolls and books of all races so that I saw how the differences of race made us all unique. I am proud to be African American and my family's history. My great-grandparents of my mother's side of the family were always referenced to as "the Perdue's." My great-aunts and great-uncles faces lit up when they reminisce on childhood experiences and vacations with their parents. I think most of my confidence within my race has been built through seeing all of the accomplishments of my great-grandparents, grandparents, and their siblings. It's funny because as a kid, I have always put my great-grandparents on this pedestal and thought of their history as the start of this dynasty.

My great-grandfather created his own janitorial business, while my great-grandmother was a homemaker. They always prioritized the importance of education and wanted all of their five children to go to college. My family gives me the motivation and desire to enjoy learning. It's one thing to hear about their history, but to share meals in the same kitchen and run in the lawn their children once played in is unreal. My great-aunt Brenda bought their house after they passed away and still holds all of our family gatherings there. She always holds brunches and dinners during different holidays. Traditions like these have taught me the importance of family, and I yearn for my future spouse to have a huge family.

My mother's parents have had even bigger, influential roles. My grandfather fought in the Vietnam War as a sniper. He received so many medals and I have always been so proud of him, as not many African Americans could be snipers. It is because of him that I can appreciate men of service and understand the effects of PTSD. I can remember doing many interviews highlighting his perspective of war and creating projects about his service. I truly love my grandfather, as there is nothing, he would not do for me. On an entirely different level, my grandmother is why I cook, as she fueled this passion of mine. As a child, I was always in awe of her. She knew just how much to add and was a fearless woman in the kitchen. She would cook lunch for her brothers and their coworkers every week, and I got to help. We would spend all morning cooking and then go deliver the plates. My grandmother's biological name was Dorothy, but to me she was "Grandmas." The holidays we spent together would be my happiest days of the year. Every

Thanksgiving, we would go grocery shopping together and spend the entire day cooking for the family. Every Christmas Eve, we would cook again, and she would spend the night with me so we could open presents together the next morning. She would always make brownies and cakes that I could send to my teachers for the holidays. If there is anything I wish I could have done, it would have been to write a cookbook with her. I always find myself trying to remember her recipes, but the food never tastes the same. My Grandmas had the magic touch, and I know that she would be so proud of me. She will forever be the reason that I love to cook and reach other people. I hate that my sister won't have the moments I had with our grandmother, but I hope that I am able to teach her a lot through cooking.

Even though I have a younger sister, I have grown up most of my life as an only child. I always wanted to be a big sister, so at the age of thirteen, I was quite shocked that I was finally going to get my chance. My mother had a lot of trouble with carrying full-term and had many miscarriages during the process. I researched her condition and through this entire process, I realized I wanted to help other people with difficult pregnancies. I want to be an OB-GYN that specializes in maternal-fetal medicine. Although the journey was hard, the birth of my sister made it all worth it. She is my current influence, as I am learning how to be a better role model for her and exercise patience. I am learning that the time we have together now is what is important, so I should focus on our relationship now and not later. I hope to be an influential part of her life and inspire her the way my past has inspired me. I look forward to the future and what my next steps in life hold. I hope to embrace this next step in life with confidence and excitement. I have never been this far away from home, but I am excited to see what the next four years in Virginia will hold.

References

Centers of Disease Control and Prevention (2016). About the CDC- Kaiser ACES Study. Retrieved on 4/25/20. from cdc.gov/violenceprevention/childabusea ndneglect/ace-study/about.html.

Center for Early Childhood Mental Health Consultation (2020). Taking Care of Ourselves: Stress Reduction Worshop. Georgetown University. Retrieved from https://www.ecmhc.org\documents\.TakingCareNotesfinalpdf.

Cuddy, E., & Reeves, R. V. (2014). "Hitting kids: American parenting and physical punishment." Retrieved on 4/25/2020 from brookings.edu/research/hitting kids- American-parenting-and physical-punishment/.

Kramer,S. (2019). U.S. Has World's Highest Rate of Children Living in Single -Parent Household. Retrieved on 8/9/2020 from https://www.pewresearch.org/fact-tank\2019\12\12\u-s-children-more-likely-than-children-in-other-countries-to-live-with-just-one-parent\?amp=1

McLeod, S. (2018). Simply Psychology. Maslow's Hierarcy of Needs. Retrieved from https://www.simplypsychology.org\maslow.html.

Libermann, A. F., Pardon, E., Vanhorn, P., & Harris W.W. (2005). "Angels in the Nursery: The Intergenerational Transmission of Benevolent Parental Influence." Infant Mental Health Journal, Vol 26 (6): 504-520.

Standard Rainbow Study Bible (2012). Standard Publishing Holy Bible, New International Version.

Substance Abuse and Mental Health Administration. (2020). Recognitizing and Treating Chld Traumatic Stress retrieved on 8/9/2020 from https:\\www.samhsa.gov/child-trauma\recognizing-and-treating-child-traumatic-stress#types. You Version Bible App. (2020). Contemporary English Version.

CPSIA information can be obtained
at www.ICGtesting.com
Printed in the USA
BVHW020723040321
601694BV00005B/15